FINDING
Your Work-Life Balance
Practical Tools for Exceptional Leaders

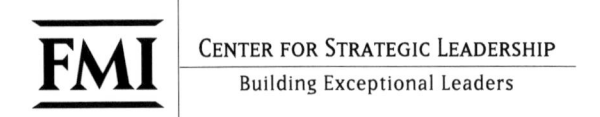

FMI | Center for Strategic Leadership
Building Exceptional Leaders

Practical Tools for Exceptional Leaders

Aimed at providing leaders with practical and transferable tools for self-development and developing other leaders.

FINDING YOUR WORK-LIFE BALANCE

Center for Strategic Leadership

Series Editor:
Mark Hooey

Copyright © 2013 FMI Corporation
Notice of Rights: No part of this publication may be reproduced or transmitted in any form, or by any means, without permission from the publisher: 303.377.4740

ISBN: 0-9740117-3-8

From the Series Editor

Welcome to FMI/CSL's
"Practical Tools for Exceptional Leaders" booklet series.

The "Practical Tools for Exceptional Leaders" booklet series is designed to help you learn and apply best of class leadership principles in your life and within your organization. These tools offer a look into fundamental leadership principles and provide you with practical guidelines for taking action. The topics and content of the booklets are structured around the questions we most commonly hear during interactions with clients within our formal programs and customized consulting engagements.

Leaders are faced with many challenging questions regarding their businesses and their lives, such as:

- How am I performing as a leader?
- What am I doing to develop leaders?
- How can we attract and retain future leaders?
- How can we position the Architect, Engineering and Construction (A/E/C) industry as an attractive career opportunity for todays' rising leaders?
- What can I do to develop quality leadership throughout our organization at every level?
- How will the decisions I make today impact the success of the business decades from now?
- Am I headed in the right direction personally and professionally?
- What will be my legacy as a leader in this organization?
- How can my organization impact the A/E/C industry?

FMI's Center for Strategic Leadership is dedicated to coaching, consulting, teaching and leading clients to examine themselves and their organizations through a leadership lens. By engaging our clients in discussions around these questions and providing valuable insight, we help them discover answers and solutions that work.

Our philosophy on leadership is that exceptional leaders are committed to continuous learning and growth. This requires that leaders learn about themselves, seek opportunities to grow and actively support the development of others. That's why we've focused these booklets on leadership fundamentals and designed them to make it easy for you to turn ideas into actions. You are on the path to exceptional leadership. Congratulations on taking this important step.

Sincerely,

Mark Hooey

Mark Hooey, Series Editor
FMI: Center for Strategic Leadership
303.398.7208
mhooey@fminet.com

Contents:

FINDING YOUR WORK-LIFE BALANCE

Who Should Use This Booklet? 1
Connection to Leadership 1
Craig's Story 3
Where Did it Fall Apart? 4
External Forces 5
Internal Forces 9
What Does Your Dash Represent? 15
Personal Dashboard 16
Building a Healthier Work-Life Balance 20
Discover the Power of Pace 29
Experience the Power of Pause 30
The Rewards 31
Notes 32

Practical Tools for Exceptional Leaders

Who Should Use This Booklet

This booklet is designed for leaders who are struggling to find their work-life balance. If you are frustrated by trying to balance work and the rest of your life in this fast-paced and chaotic life, then you will find the advice and instruction in this booklet useful.

Connection to Leadership

Learning to focus your attention, time and energy on the important areas and roles in life is critical to being an effective leader and finding your work-life balance. You will feel more satisfied with your life when you are "balanced". The more satisfied you feel, the better you will respond to the people and world around you.

FMI's Center for Strategic Leadership uses the Peak Leaders Model to illustrate the key categories and behaviors that are critical for overall leader success. We call this the Peak Leaders Model because we feel that every person has leadership potential. The level of potential varies from person to person just as athletic potential varies. Our goal is for every person to maximize his or her unique leadership potential. We want you to reach your "peak" leadership potential.

The outside ring is segmented into eight categories. Each category is a discipline behavior area that leaders should become proficient in to maximize their leadership and reach their peak potential. You probably know many successful leaders who were very good at some of these behaviors but very poor at others. You may have moved up in your organization because you mastered one or more of these discipline behavior areas. However, to realize your peak potential as a leader, you must develop in each of the discipline behavior areas.

We believe "Finding Your Work-Life Balance" belongs in the Lead Within behavior of the model. To be effective in leading from within, leaders need to live their personal mission and values, understand their definition of success, manage their time and energy and have healthy practices and routines.

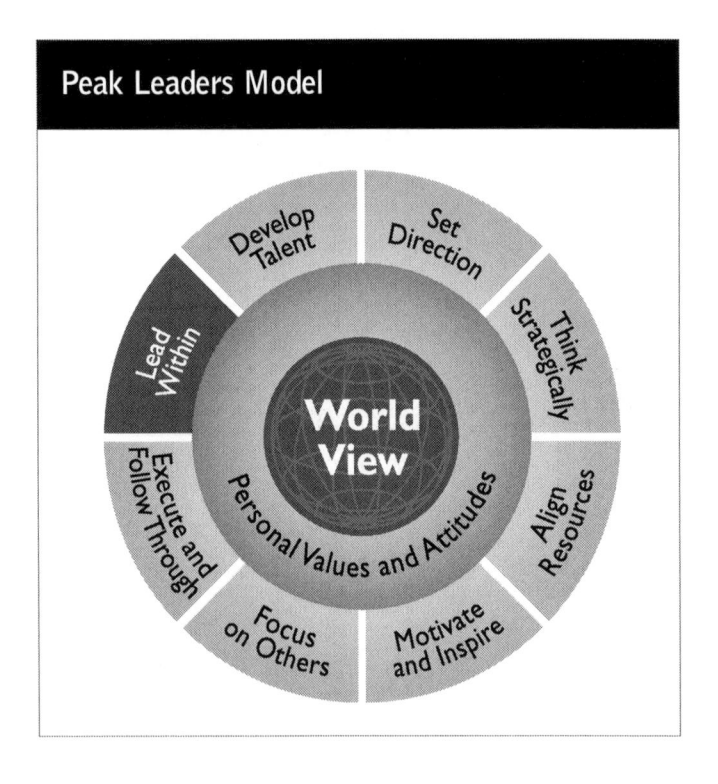

Peak Leaders Model

- Develop Talent
- Set Direction
- Think Strategically
- Align Resources
- Motivate and Inspire
- Focus on Others
- Execute and Follow Through
- Lead Within

Center: World View / Personal Values and Attitudes

Craig's Story

Craig Parker is a 41-year-old senior project manager for a large commercial builder based in the Midwest region of the United States. Craig loves his job — the satisfaction of meaningful work, being part of a great team and adding value to his clients. His company has been good to him, allowing him to grow and develop his skills and supporting him, even when he makes mistakes. His compensation is more than fair; in fact, it would be hard to match, if he decided to work elsewhere.

He works hard like most people in his industry. Most days you will find him on the job by 6:30 a.m., and he frequently does not get home until 8:00 p.m. Most Saturdays he works at least half a day — "just to catch up," he tells himself. Honestly, it has been a long time since he's felt caught up.

Craig has been married for 15 years and has two children, seven and 10 years old. He loves his family and feels guilty because he is not able to give them as much attention as he would like. His wife, Holly, has been supportive of his career and enjoys the lifestyle his income allows, but for a while now, she has made it known that she feels all alone when it comes to parenting. It has been too long since they have felt connected, and Craig secretly wonders if his marriage is in trouble.

His doctor lectured him at his last appointment because his weight, blood pressure and cholesterol are reaching unhealthy levels. It was evident that too many meals on the run, no time for exercise and nonstop stress were taking a toll on his health.

By the end of a project, after too many long days and sleepless nights, he has found himself feeling resentful about the pressure he is under. Although he feels lucky to have a job, sometimes Craig feels like this unhealthy cycle will never end.

> *"It takes more than work to feel satisfied in life."*

Craig is representative of many of FMI's clients — smart, successful, diligent and driven. Increasingly though, many are starting to realize that if they do not find some balance, their families, health and general well-being will continue to decline.

The common concern is that if they slow down for even a minute, they will lose their edge. We see this so frequently that we consider it a predictable step in the leadership-development process. Finding your work-life balance will be a launching pad for greater effectiveness in the workplace and increased satisfaction with life in general.

Where did it fall apart?

Work is an important part of life. It provides us with more than an income. It gives shape to our days, contributes to our sense of purpose and allows us to feel a pride in being part of something bigger than ourselves.

When work consumes the majority of our time, it takes a toll on our physical and emotional health, hinders our ability to make wise decisions and puts a strain on our relationships. Sharon L. Allen, Chairman of the Board at Deloitte and Touche USA recently said, "When you think about it, if someone invests all their time and energy into their jobs, it may have the unintended consequence of making them dependent on their jobs for everything — including their sense of self-worth. This makes it even harder to make a good choice when faced with an ethical dilemma, if they believe it will impact their professional success."

If we are honest with ourselves, it takes more than work to feel satisfied in life. We need our health, relationships, recreation and down time along with work to live a full life. However, many today feel those things must be sacrificed if we are to be successful in an extremely competitive industry.

> *"Just because many people are doing it, doesn't make it right or good."*

You can find plenty of examples of people sacrificing their health, relationships and recreation. They are working a lot of hours each week trying to be successful. Just because many people are doing it doesn't make it right or good. It only means many people are struggling with work-life balance.

We have heard many stories of people struggling with work-life balance, and there are many stories of people making positive life changes that create better balance, health and well-being. You, too, can find your work-life balance, but it may mean swimming against a current of powerful forces of contemporary expectations and examples.

External forces

Before we get to the solution-side of this challenge, let's look at how work has evolved into the all-consuming focus for so many smart, successful people.

1. **The undertow of expectations**

   Anyone who has spent time at a beach knows an undertow is a powerful current — often not visible from the surface — that can pull an unsuspecting person far from shore so quickly he or she does not even notice until he or she is in trouble.

   That is how it often feels in the workplace these days. Every year, the hours and responsibilities increase and so does the pressure that "everyone has to do this to be successful."

In an article entitled "Extreme Jobs", authors Hewlett and Luce document the rise of employees whose jobs are characterized by:

- Unpredictable flow of work
- Fast-paced work under tight deadlines
- Inordinate scope of work that amounts to more than one job
- Work-related events outside regular work hours
- Availability to clients 24/7
- Responsibility for profit and loss
- Responsibility for mentoring and recruiting
- Large amount of travel
- Large number of reports
- Physical presence at the workplace (at least 10 hours a day)

The overwhelming majority of extreme jobholders in this study love their jobs. As quoted in the article, "Extreme Jobs", "Far from seeing themselves as workaholics in need of rescuing, extreme workers wear their commitments like a badge of honor."

Yet these same extreme workers admit that their jobs take a toll on their health and relationships with spouses and children.

Clearly, what some have called the American dream on steroids comes with a significant downside.

Reflect and Respond: Have external expectations negatively influenced my life? Is there anything I need to do differently?

_____

_____

_____

2. **Fatigue**

    If some of us drove our vehicles the way we drive ourselves, we would be sitting on the side of the road with an empty gas tank and a dead battery waiting for a tow truck.

    Yet that is frequently the kind of pressure we put on ourselves, especially on projects with tight deadlines and tighter margins. If a person gives everything he or she has, every single day, eventually the body and mind rebel through illness, breakdown or burnout.

    When people are conscientious about work and family, they often cheat themselves by sleeping less. There is a common belief during crunch time that an hour less sleep computes to an hour of added productivity. Unfortunately, research shows a significant loss in productivity from sleep-deprived employees.

    Sleeping less than six hours a night is one of the greatest predictors of burnout. It is worth noting that Amnesty International considers sleep deprivation to be a form of torture.

    Knowing when to stop before the tank runs dry and knowing how to refill the tank are some of the skills that can lead us back to healthy living.

Reflect and Respond: Is fatigue negatively affecting my life? Is there anything I need to do differently?

_____

_____

_____

_____

3. **The digital deception**

   There is no question access to digital tools (i.e., smartphones, tablets and laptops) has increased our productivity. We are no longer chained to a desk. We can set up shop just about anywhere we have a cell signal or wireless access.

   Technology has led to greater safety, better risk management and a host of other benefits.

   The downside is that being available all the time has taken something valuable from us — the ability to mentally and physically disconnect. When we leave the office, we don't leave work and are unable to switch to a healthier pace.

   The expectation that a person should be available to the client and the boss 24/7 is increasingly becoming the norm. Sometimes this expectation is self-imposed. Being the master and not the slave of technology has become a bigger challenge with every new technological development.

Reflect and Respond: Am I the master or the slave of technology? How can I be more effective in this area?

_____

_____

_____

_____

_____

Internal forces

The 19th century humorist Josh Billings often said, "The trouble ain't what people don't know; it's what they know that ain't so." Most of us believe things that are not necessarily true. Consider some of the following myths concerning work, and notice whether or not you believe them to be true.

1. **"More is better"**
   In 1979, the U.S. Army Corps of Engineers published "The Modification Impact Evaluation Guide". The most significant finding in this study was how efficiency declines at a fairly steep rate as people worked more hours per day and more days per week. In other words, the relationship between number of work hours per day and days per week and efficiency does not remain constant.

   Somewhere between 40-50 hours a week, most people find their "sweet spot" of productivity. As you can see from the graph, efficiency diminishes quickly as the number of hours increase.

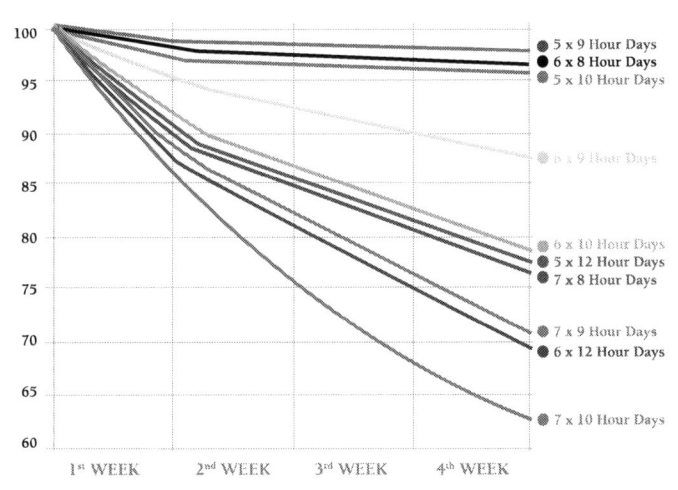

   Modification Impact Evaluation Guide
   U.S. Army Corps of Engineers

Reflect and Respond: How could I set better work-hour limits for others and myself, and remain productive?

2. **"I'm the only one who can do it"**
   Conscientious people take pride in their work and want to be sure everything is perfect. We all have limits of how much we can produce by ourselves.

   Due to effort and quality of work, individuals are often promoted to levels where they are personally doing less hands-on work and are supervising others who produce the tangible products or services. This sets up a trap for leaders with perfectionistic tendencies. They struggle with delegating tasks because they believe they are the only ones that can do a task correctly.

   Leaders can work harder and longer doing everything themselves, or they can begin to delegate tasks they would rather hang on to. Delegating will help leaders reach significantly higher levels of production and accomplishment than they will ever achieve by themselves. Delegating is a terrific way of developing people as well as assisting leaders to obtain a better work-life balance. If you would like more information on how to delegate effectively, you can refer to our "Delegating for Leader Development" booklet in this series.

Reflect and Respond: Do I believe I am the only one who can do it? If so, what are the underlying fears that fuel this belief?

_____

_____

_____

_____

_____

_____

Reflect and Respond: Do I believe I am the only one that can do it? If so, what impact is this having on my work-life balance?

_____

_____

_____

_____

_____

_____

Reflect and Respond: Am I hesitant to trust others with key skills, tasks or information? If so, how does this affect me delegating to others?

_____
_____
_____
_____
_____
_____
_____

Reflect and Respond: How does my delegating benefit me? How does my delegating benefit the ones to whom I am delegating?

_____
_____
_____
_____
_____
_____
_____

3. **"I have to pull my weight"**
    Most of our clients got where they are because they have a track record of results-oriented dependability. We affirm the desire to be a productive member of a highly functional team; however, the challenge we face is when our self-expectation exceeds company expectations and causes us to take on more than we can effectively handle. This worldview and behavior may hinder our ability to have a healthy work-life balance and make it difficult to discern when enough is enough.

> Internal forces or worldviews usually operate below the level of consciousness.

Reflect and Respond: Do I believe I have to pull my weight? If so, how has this belief hindered my work-life balance?

_____

_____

_____

_____

_____

_____

_____

Reflect and Respond: In regards to pulling my weight, do my self-expectations align with company expectations?" If not, how have these self-expectations affected my work-life balance?

_____

_____

_____

_____

_____

Reflect and Respond: Do I jump in and get it done to the detriment of allowing others to grow and have the satisfaction of contributing? If so, how might I handle this differently in the future?

_____

_____

_____

_____

_____

These internal forces or worldviews usually operate below the level of consciousness. Identifying them is a necessary step to being able to make positive changes in your work-life balance.

What does your dash represent?

"The 'Dash' represents everything we think, say and do in our lives."

Picture a headstone standing in a row in a cemetery. Beneath the name of the deceased, you will find two dates. The first usually refers to birth and the second refers to death. Between those dates, you will find a little symbol, the dash. The dash is more important than the dates on either side because it represents everything a person thinks, says and does from the day he or she is born until the day he or she dies. When a person dies, a memorial service is held. It is a time to reflect on what that person accomplished in life. Stories are told of the person's life accomplishments — what is in his or her dash.

Every person gets to decide how to use the days allotted to him or her — what he or she wants in his or her dash. Some want to build an empire. Others want to leave a legacy. Some want to leave the world better than when they found it. Some never get around to making plans, and in the blink of an eye, their life is gone.

No one ever said from his or her deathbed, "I wish I'd spent more time at work." Taking time now to contemplate how you want to live your life gives you the chance to minimize regrets before it is too late.

The average life expectancy in the United States for men is about 76 years (27,750 days). Women live about 81 years (29,575 days). This means we only have a few short years to build our dash. What is in your dash? What would you like in your dash?

Your Personal Dashboard

HEALTH   FAMILY   FRIENDS

CAREER   COMMUNITY   LEARNING

We have a couple of activities to help you identify what you would like in your dash.

Personal Dashboard

Imagine that your life has a dashboard with gauges, just like a high-performance automobile. Each gauge represents a major area or role in your life. How would you label the major areas or roles in your life? In no particular order, here are some suggested areas or roles.

- Career
- Spiritual
- Fun
- Friends
- Personal health
- Learning
- Community
- Family

Practical Tools for Exceptional Leaders

Identify the six major areas or roles in your life. Label each of the six gauges above. After labeling the gauges, draw a needle representing how "full" each gauge would read. If you had to force rank these areas, what order or priority would you give them? Do you determine the order/priority by time and energy spent, or do you use which feels more important. Does the time and energy you devote to each area equate to the level of importance in your life? If you could measure your current level of satisfaction or success in each major area of your life, how would your gauges read? Full, half full or empty? Ask yourself a few questions to help you know how to read your gauges: What does it take to get a gauge to read full? What causes a gauge to read empty? How do you know when your gauges are full or empty?

Once you identify your satisfaction or success level in each area or role, you will better understand why particular areas of your life seem more or less stressful.

Pay attention to which areas of your life cause you anxiety or guilt, and ask yourself why. Would the other important people in your life agree or disagree with your assessment? What would your kids, spouse, friends, family, direct reports, co-workers or manager say about your priorities?

Have compassion with yourself. This is just an assessment — none of us is perfect at everything! An accurate assessment is crucial to developing a personal strategy for change.

Reflect and Respond:
- What was it like to complete this exercise?
- Where did you struggle?
- Would it be worth conducting a "Family Satisfaction Survey"?
- How well are you maintaining your most important relationships?
- What happens if all your roles involve taking care of others?
- Do you need to take care of yourself first to succeed in every other role?
- How does this exercise relate to what you put in your dash?
- How will this exercise help you create a healthier work-life balance?
- Does giving more time and energy to an area equate to more satisfaction or success or create a healthier balance?

_____

_____

_____

_____

Building a healthier work-life balance

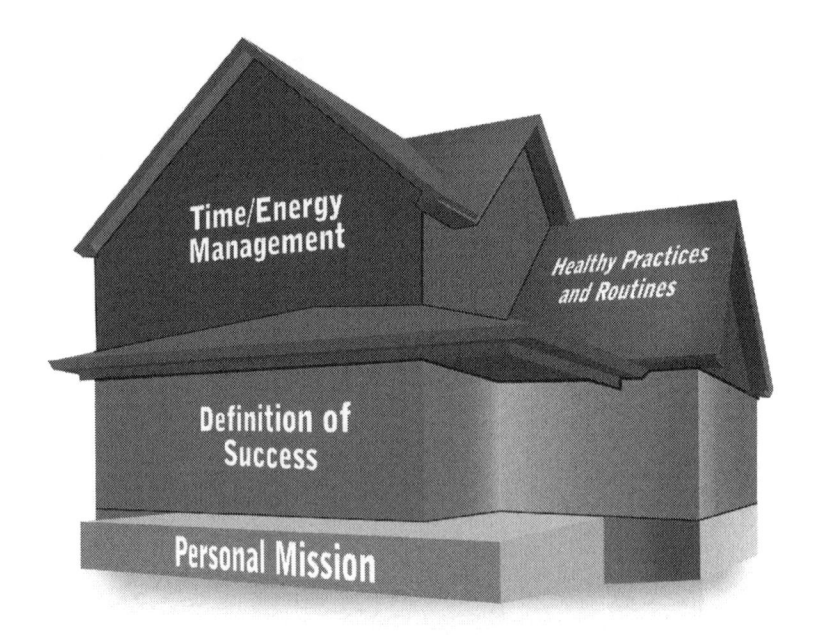

[Diagram of a house with labels: Time/Energy Management, Healthy Practices and Routines, Definition of Success, Personal Mission]

Now it is time to construct a development plan and build a healthier work-life balance.

A healthy work-life balance is like a well-built structure or house. A solid foundation is essential and must be laid before the walls can be constructed. The second story can only be laid after the first story is framed. The roof comes last and ties everything together. Let's look at this model one step at a time.

1. **Identify or reconnect with your core values and personal mission**
   Just like a building or house, every leader needs a solid foundation on which to stand if he or she is going to thrive in this chaotic world. Every leader should answer the question, what centers me?

Knowing your core values and having a sense of purpose will provide a stable place from which you can lead effectively.

First, identify your "core" values. The clearer you are about your core values, the easier it is to make difficult decisions. The more your decisions and values coincide, the more satisfying your life will become. Take a moment and brainstorm all the things and ideas you value. Some may be tangible, like family, friends, work and hobbies, while others may be intangible, like honesty, integrity, loyalty and love. List as many as you can and then identify your top seven values. After identifying your top seven values, put them in order with No. 1 being the thing or idea you value most.

_____

_____

_____

_____

_____

_____

_____

_____

_____

"Why am I on this Earth?"

Now that you identified and prioritized your values, ask yourself the tough questions. How am I doing at living my values? Am I making decisions (home and work) that closely align with my values? Am I responding to people and events around me based on my values, or am I responding from my emotions and frustration I feel from the chaotic world in which I live? The more closely our behaviors align with our values, the more satisfied we will be with our lives. The further apart our behaviors are from our values, the less satisfied we are with our lives.

Next, identify your personal mission. A way of discovering your personal mission is by asking, "Why am I on this earth?" While this question may seem philosophical, it is worth pondering. Each person should answer this question for him or herself. If he or she does not, then he or she will likely follow the path provided by something or someone else. Although this may not be all bad, it may take him or her down a path that does not align well with his or her personal values.

If you would like to take a deeper dive into developing your personal mission statement, get a copy of our "Developing Your Mission Statement" booklet in the Practical Tools For Exceptional Leaders Booklet Series.

Reflect and Respond: Why am I here? What do I want to accomplish with my life? What is my legacy? As you answer these questions, consider all the major areas and roles in your life (i.e., work, family, hobbies, etc.).

_____

_____

_____

_____

_____

_____

_____

_____

_____

Knowing what we stand for, believe in and value most is an important first step to laying the foundation for building a balanced life. The more our actions align with our personal mission and values, the more satisfied we will be with our lives. The more satisfied we are with our life direction, the better we will respond to people and the world around us. We believe finding your work-life balance must begin with identifying your core values and personal mission.

2. **Clarify your personal definition of success**

   After the foundation is complete, the ground floor can be built. We believe your definition of success is the ground floor. Your definition of success is what drives and influences your behaviors from the moment you wake, until the moment you go to sleep. Most of us roll out of bed and immediately begin thinking about our day. We usually think about everything we have to accomplish that day. There will be tasks that will carry over to the next day and week, but we are figuring out how we can be successful today. We want to be successful in whatever we do. Very few, if any, people get up in the morning with the intent of failing at everything they do.

   There is a story of Alexander the Great in India. He encountered a group of monks sitting in meditation in the middle of the road next to the Indus River. As Alexander's party tried to get through, the monks would not move.

   Finally, one of Alexander's zealous, young lieutenants tried to get them to move by verbally abusing them. As he was chewing out an older monk, Alexander himself came to the front. Pointing to Alexander, the young lieutenant screamed, "This man has conquered the world! What have you accomplished?

   The monk looked up calmly and replied, "I have conquered the need to conquer the world."

"…energy, not time, is the fundamental currency of high performance."

Alexander roared with laughter. "Could I be any man in the world other than myself, I would be this man," he said.

Your definition of success will probably change with the different stages of your life. Your definition 10 years ago was probably different than it is today, and it will be different again 10 years from today. Make sure you are clear on your definition of success in all the major areas and roles of your life, as this will drive your behaviors, which will directly influence your effectiveness.

Reflect and Respond: What is my definition of success? What am I doing to be successful? How has my definition of success changed over the years? Is my definition of success consistent with my values and mission in life?

3. **Practice time and energy management**

   Most leaders have had some training in time management, and it is essential that we learn how to deal with the "Important versus Urgent." Greater productivity is not measured solely in hours spent on the job, but in results. One approach to work-life balance is to focus on ways to increase energy and focus throughout the day, while also being intentional about conserving enough energy and focus for life outside of work.

   There is a surprising paradox at work here. Instead of taking away from one's productivity at work, finding balance and integration will actually give you more energy and focus for your work.

   The following equation can help us understand this idea.

Energy + Focus = Productivity

"People don't multitask because they're good at it. They do it because they are more distracted."

—— David Sanbonmatsu

Managing energy

We all occasionally feel like we are not up to par. Upon reflection, we usually find it is the result of a bad night's sleep or the accumulation of too many long, stressful days.

In their landmark book, "The Power of Full Engagement", Jim Loehr and Tony Schwartz insist that, "... energy, not time, is the fundamental currency of high performance."

While physical energy is the type we most commonly recognize, "The Power of Full Engagement" offers practical ways to increase emotional, mental and spiritual energy as well. (In this context, spiritual does not have a religious context, but refers to an awareness of significance outside ourselves.)

Sleep management is an essential component of managing energy. There is broad scientific consensus that the majority of people need seven to eight hours of quality sleep to function optimally.

Our **diet** has a far greater impact on our energy levels than we might expect. Learning to eat the right foods at the right times can dramatically affect our energy levels.

Everyone acknowledges the importance of **exercise**. You may also have heard Paul Terry's popular response. "Whenever I feel the need to exercise, I lie down until it goes away." Achieving and maintaining a healthy level of fitness increases our energy, alertness and ability to function under stress. Exercise is so important that researchers tell us that if we have to make a choice, a half-hour of cardiovascular exercise or strength training is more desirable than an extra half-hour of sleep!

Managing focus
Focus is the ability to push aside other things for a period of time and give our singular energy to the task at hand. It is becoming such a rare commodity in our age, that those who take the time to cultivate that ability will often be rewarded in significant ways.

For many years, researchers have been making the case that people who drive while on their cell phone drive as badly as people who are legally drunk. Most of us still consider ourselves the exception to the rule.

"People don't multitask because they're good at it. They do it because they are more distracted." – David Sanbonmatsu

We may have justified our multitasking by thinking we were being more productive. The more likely reason is that we are unsure about what is the most important thing to do in the moment.

Reflect and Respond: How well am I managing my time and energy? How can I take better care of myself so I can have more energy? How can I make sure I am putting my energy in the important rather than the urgent areas? How can I better manage my stress?

4. **Develop healthy practices and routines**
   The final step in building the life you desire is to put in place healthy practices and routines.

   As we entered the workforce, we developed habits and routines we believed would help us be successful. The problem is that we were in a different life stage when we developed those habits and routines. For example, in our 20's, we were young, energetic and single. We could work long hours, survive on less sleep and pay little attention to our diet and drinking habits with little immediate effect. We were only responsible for ourselves. Time and money were ours to spend as we chose. The habits we develop at a young age tend to stick with us. Habits are hard to break; we are creatures of habit after all. However, over time, our life stages evolved, but our habits and routines remained the same. Fast-forward a few decades, and those same habits will sink our ship in a hurry.

   At each stage of life, we should evaluate our practices and routines to ensure they are still relevant and effective.

Discover the power of pace

In Formula-One racing, the world's most talented drivers must navigate the most technically difficult courses. These drivers navigate tight corners and elevation changes at speeds of more than 200 mph. Yet they cannot drive at top speed throughout the course. They must slow down at exactly the right places, or they will fail to negotiate the hairpin turns and find themselves out of the race.

In life, there are glorious stretches of the journey when you can put the pedal to the metal and experience the thrill of speed and power. However, there are also times when the pace of life must slow down, or there will be serious consequences. We need to learn to recognize the warning signs of life that tell us when sharp turns are ahead, so we can adjust our speed to be more successful. The warning signs can be external (family, friends or co-workers) or internal (health).

Experience the power of pause

Closely related to the "Power of Pace" is the "Power of Pause." The power of pace is when we increase or decrease our pace to manage our energy. The power of pause is stopping for strategic breaks and injections of fun in life to recoup energy and focus.

Productivity goes up when we take strategic breaks in our day, week, month and year. These periods of rest allow our mind to disconnect and reset, and our body to move. Remember what it was like to have recess as a kid. It is wise to occasionally come to a hard stop and let things slow down. Learning when to race ahead full throttle and when to stop completely will enhance your life in ways most of us have yet to experience.

Reflect and Respond: What practices and routines do I need to adjust in my current life stage? How can I better apply the power of pace and pause in my life?

_____

_____

_____

_____

_____

_____

The Rewards

If you find yourselves on the same path as Craig (whose story we told at the beginning of this booklet), rest assured you can make the necessary life changes and find your work-life balance.

If you do the work described in this booklet
- Identifying your personal values
- Discovering your personal mission
- Gaining clarity around your definition of success
- Effectively managing your time and energy
- Developing healthy habits and routines

You will:
- Be more satisfied with the direction of your life
- Respond better to the people and world around you
- Experience a far greater sense of control over your life
- Enjoy the freedom that comes when we learn to live in harmony with our purpose and values
- Discover the fulfillment of a well-integrated life
- Feel more content as you reconnect with family, friends and hobbies

As you have worked through this booklet, we hope you have developed a plan for living a life with new levels of satisfaction, contentment and joy. We hope you have found your work-life balance. If so, we would love to hear your story!

Notes

Notes

Notes

DEVELOPMENTAL RESOURCES

Practical Tools for Exceptional Leaders Booklets

Creating Your Leader Development Plan
Developing your leadership ability requires constant attention and effort—you can never truly be finished. Good leaders strive to continually grow, and they understand that there are always opportunities to further develop their leadership skills. *Creating Your Leader Development Plan* will provide you with a clear path to follow in developing your skills as a leader, advancing your career and assisting others in the development of their leadership skills. This booklet will lead you through a series of steps to create a plan for your development and put it to work.

Delegating for Leader Development
The ultimate job of any leader is to simultaneously advance the strategic goals and objectives of the firm and to develop the workers' skills and abilities. This booklet focuses on learning to do just that through intentional, purposeful and personal delegation.

Developing Your Mission Statement
Knowing your purpose in life is critical to your professional and personal development. A personal mission statement provides you with a compass—pointing in the direction you should go. This booklet is designed for leaders who are seeking clarity in the direction and purpose of their professional and personal life.

Giving and Receiving Feedback
Giving and Receiving Feedback is a powerful tool that will help develop the necessary skills to fully utilize feedback as a means of self-knowledge as well as empowering others to perform at their highest levels. This booklet will help you to increase the performance of those you work with, as well as increasing your own leadership effectiveness.

Clarifying Your World View
One of the most critical competencies of effective leaders is the ability to understand and adapt to the manner in which others see the world. A leader must first uncover and understand how his or her worldview influences his or her behavior. A great leader will know when a worldview is helping or getting in the way of being effective.

Order Form

Item	Price	Qty	Subtotal
☐ I would like to order additional copies of **Finding Your Work-Life Balance**	$14.95		
I would like to order other Practical Tools for Exceptional Leaders Booklets			
☐ Clarifying Your Worldview	$14.95		
☐ Delegating for Leader Development	$14.95		
☐ Creating Your Leader Development Plan	$14.95		
☐ Developing Your Mission Statement	$14.95		
☐ Giving and Receiving Feedback	$14.95		
Add sales tax if resident of NC (7%), CO (7.2%), FL (6%)			
U.S. shipping & handling (add 5%, with a min. of $2.95) Non-U.S. shipping (add 40%, with a minimum of $8) Express shipping service available on orders placed over the phone.			
		TOTAL	

☐ CHECK HERE to receive information about FMI's Leadership programs

☐ Payment Enclosed (Make checks payable to FMI)

Bill my: ☐ Mastercard ☐ Visa ☐ AMEX

Acct# Signature Exp. Date

Name Title

Company

City State Zip

Daytime Phone email Fax

To order, complete and return a copy of this form or contact us at:

FMI, 5171 Glenwood Ave., Suite 200, Raleigh, NC 27612
P 919.787.8400 | F 919.785.9320 | Online www.fminet.com/csl.html

FMI's Leadership Development Programs

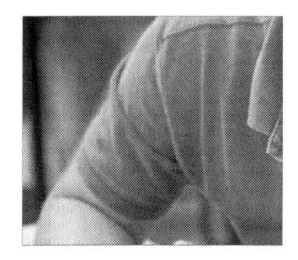

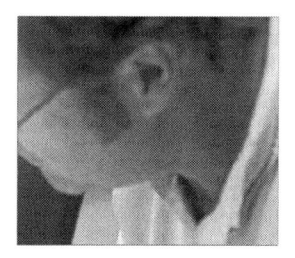

Executive Coaching:
Developing Your Leadership Skills

Who holds you accountable for improving your ability to lead?
Who guides you through difficult leadership, personal and career decisions?

Study after study confirms that long-term, periodic professional coaching is the only way to create sustainable leadership growth.

Executive Coaching is a one-on-one partnership between you and your FMI professional coach to meet your specialized needs and goals. Our FMI coaches bring specialized knowledge gained from more than 60 years of management consulting to the construction industry.

We strive to provide coaching that is:
- Specifically tailored to help you execute workplace strategies
- Built around your work experiences and challenges
- Distinctively designed to help you leverage your abilities within your organization

FMI'S LEADERSHIP DEVELOPMENT PROGRAMS

Who uses FMI's Executive Coaching? Professional coaching is ideal for any middle or senior level leader interested in accelerating his or her leadership development. Our coaching clients consist of CEOs, presidents, vice presidents, operations managers, project managers, senior estimators, senior superintendents and others who are committed to maximizing their leadership potential.

In addition, several of our larger client companies also use FMI's **Executive Coaching** as part of a custom program to develop their next generation of leaders.

To register for this program and for more information:

Call 303.398.7209
or visit
www.fminet.com/coaching

FMI's Leadership Development Programs

Leadership Institute
Building Exceptional Leaders

FMI Leadership Institute is a tightly structured four-day program in which industry professionals examine themselves and their organizations through a variety of hands-on experiences.

The program focuses on five main areas:

1. Personal assessment and individual development
2. Experiential leadership opportunities
3. A small-group construction company simulation
4. Giving and receiving effective feedback
5. Essentials of leadership for the future of the construction/design industry

Benefits of Attending:

Organizational

- Lower the risk of your business by building a deep pipeline of leaders
- Enhance your ability to execute strategic growth initiatives
- Increase engagement and organizational loyalty
- Develop the capacity for your organization's leaders to step into roles of greater responsibility and impact
- Equip your organization with the leadership talent needed to make the right strategic moves in a changing economy

Individual

- Learn how you can reach your peak potential as a leader
- Gain a deeper understanding of your leadership strengths and opportunities for growth through personal aptitude, personality and 360° feedback assessments
- Obtain a clearer understanding of your leadership effectiveness from coaching and feedback from Institute staff and industry peers
- Discover specific "next steps" to improving your leadership performance from a personal plan of action
- Advance your professional development when you receive a certificate of completion for continuing education credits

To register for this program and for more information:

Call 303.398.7221
or visit
www.fminet.com/leadershipinstitute

About FMI's Center for Strategic Leadership (CSL)

We Are...
FMI's Center for Strategic Leadership is dedicated to building a better future for the Architect, Engineering and Construction (A/E/C) Industry by developing exceptional leaders, one at a time. We offer customized leadership development services specifically designed to work within the unique context of the A/E/C Industry. By blending extensive industry knowledge and in-depth leadership experience, the CSL is able to develop successful solutions to industry problems. We deliver on-site programs that introduce leadership concepts, foster dialogue on leadership issues, generate realistic solutions to leadership challenges and create opportunities for skill building and real-time feedback.

We Have...
- Helped leaders from across the globe navigate the challenges of our ever-changing environment
- Graduated more than 4000 participants from our world class Leadership Institute
- Provided Executive Coaching since 2003 helping more than 250 leaders achieve greater results
- Worked with 4 out of the top 6 contractors in Fortune's 100 Best Companies to work for
- Provided 35% of ENR's Top 400 Contractors with leadership development services

We Provide...
The CSL gives clients the confidence and assurance that comes with developing their most important resource—people. We strive to serve as a trusted advisor to our clients by...

- Building great organizations that last for generations
- Gaining competitive advantage with business savvy leaders
- Increasing clarity on strategic decisions
- Increasing engagement and retention through leadership development
- Preserving the organizational culture for the next generation
- Increasing capacity to focus on strategic issues
- Identifying and developing future leaders
- Clarifying management succession plans
- Understanding the effects of global dynamics on the business
- Strengthening executive team's thinking
- Shaping cultures of excellence

We Do...
- Individual and Team Assessments
- Individual Leader Development
- Leadership Transition
- Strategic Leadership
- Speaking Engagements

We Offer...
- Leadership Institute
- Executive Coaching
- Organizational Leadership Development
- Leadership Training

About FMI

FMI is a leading provider of management consulting, investment banking† and research to the engineering and construction industry. We work in all segments of the industry providing clients with value-added business solutions, including:

- Strategic Advisory
- Market Research and Business Development
- Leadership and Talent Development
- Project and Process Improvement
- Mergers, Acquisitions and Financial Consulting†
- Compensation Benchmarking and Consulting
- Risk Management Consulting

Founded by Dr. Emol A. Fails in 1953, FMI has professionals in offices across the U.S. We deliver innovative, customized solutions to contractors, construction materials producers, manufacturers and suppliers of building materials and equipment, owners and developers, engineers and architects, utilities, and construction industry trade associations. FMI is an advisor you can count on to build and maintain a successful business, from your leadership to your site managers.

† *Investment banking services provided by FMI Capital Advisors, Inc., a registered broker-dealer and wholly owned subsidiary of FMI.*

FMI

www.fminet.com

BUILDING A BETTER FUTURE FOR THE
CONSTRUCTION INDUSTRY
BY DEVELOPING EXCEPTIONAL LEADERS,
ONE AT A TIME.

Raleigh
5171 Glenwood Avenue
Suite 200
Raleigh, NC 27612
T 919.787.8400
F 919.785.9320

Denver
210 University Boulevard
Suite 800
Denver, CO 80206
T 303.377.4740
F 303.398.7291

Tampa
308 South Boulevard
Tampa, FL 33606
T 813.636.1364
F 813.636.9601

Scottsdale
14500 N. Northsight Boulevard
Suite 313
Scottsdale, AZ 85260
T 602.381.8108
F 602.381.8228

www.fmicsl.com

FMI
Sixty Years

Made in the USA
Columbia, SC
06 June 2017